PHOENICIAN CIVILIZATION

ANCIENT HISTORY FOR KIDS

ANCIENT SEMITIC THALASSOCRATIC CIVILIZATION
5TH GRADE SOCIAL STUDIES

BABY PROFESSOR
EDUCATION KIDS

Speedy Publishing LLC

40 E. Main St. #1156

Newark, DE 19711

www.speedypublishing.com

Copyright 2017

In this book, we're going to talk about the Phoenician Civilization. So, let's get right to it!

WHAT WAS PHOENICIA?

The ancient civilization of Phoenicia was composed of city-states that were positioned along the Mediterranean coastline. The part of the coastline they occupied is today sections of the country of Syria, the country of Lebanon, and the northern region of Israel.

Tyre, which was an island city, and Sidon were most influential of the city-states, while Baalbek and Byblos were the religious hubs. Byblos was the Greek name for the Phoenician city of Gebal. These regions of population began around 3200 BC and were well-established 500 years later. From the years 1500 BC to 332 BC, the Phoenician civilization was at its peak both as a sea trader as well as a center for manufacturing.

The Phoenician people were skilled in many different industries:

- The construction and design of beautiful sea-worthy ships

- The invention of innovative navigational tools
- The production of color dyes, especially royal purple

The Phoenicians and
The First Alphabet

- The manufacture of both common and luxury goods
- The creation of glass
- The design of the alphabet, which eventually evolved into the alphabet that most Western languages use today

PHOENICIAN SHIPS

The Phoenicians were known for their ships. They built two different types of ships. Their "gauloi" also known as "round ships" were constructed with hulls that were rounded and sterns that were curved.

The gauloi had massive rectangular sails positioned at their centers. These sails could turn to take the best advantage of the wind. A blade that was like an oar at the left or port side of the ship was used to steer.

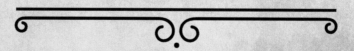

Their warships were designed differently. They had two sails and there were coverings positioned on deck to shield the officers. The front or bow of the ship had an area where catapults were used. This area was called the forecastle. The warships were also equipped with a tip made of bronze on the front of the ship. This tip was called a "rostrum" and was used as a "battering ram" against other ships.

ASSYRIAN WARSHIP

The Phoenician ships had interesting decorations. They had eyes that were painted on to provide a magical way for the ship to "see." These giant eyes were designed to scare enemies too. Perhaps the

most distinctive decoration was the giant horse head on the front of the ship. It was designed to honor Yamm, the sea god and the brother of the god of death, Mot.

The style of ships that the Phoenicians created was very sophisticated. Long after their empire had declined, both the Greeks and the Romans copied their design. The Phoenicians also invented many different tools to help with navigation. It's believed that they may have been the first to thoroughly survey the Mediterranean Sea. They were also the first people from the Mediterranean to brave sailing in the vast Atlantic Ocean.

ANCIENT PHOENICIA WAS A SEMITIC AND THALASSOCRATIC CIVILIZATION

The ancient civilization of Phoenicia was populated by Semitic people. The term "Semitic" means people who spoke ancient languages that originated from the lands between Africa and Asia. One of these languages was the ancient Phoenician. The ancient Akkadian language was also a Semitic language as are Hebrew, Aramaic and Arabic.

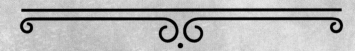

A nother term that describes ancient Phoenicia is "Thalassocratic." Thalassocratic means that they were sailors and their economy was built on their ability to trade their goods by traveling over the seas.

PURPLE POWDER DYE

THE PURPLE PEOPLE

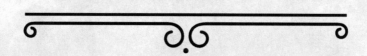

T he word Phoenician comes from the Greek word "Phoinikes," which was the word for the rich-looking purple dye made by the Tyranians. The purple dye was used for royalty and the kings from the empire of Mesopotamia bought their robes from the Phoenicians.

The famous Greek historian Herodotus wrote that the people were called that because they manufactured this dye, but

also because it stained their skin making them "purple people."

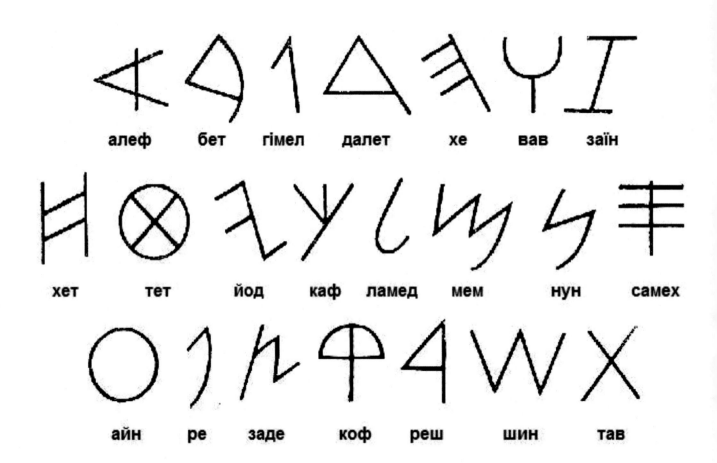

алеф   бет   гімел   далет   хе   вав   заїн

хет   тет   йод   каф   ламед   мем   нун   самех

айн   ре   заде   коф   реш   шин   тав

THE PHOENICIAN ALPHABET

The symbols of the Phoenician alphabet don't look recognizable as our modern alphabet but they were the beginnings of it. The word "phonics" comes from "Phoenician." It was the first writing system that was based on sounds and it was the first alphabet.

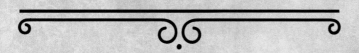

Because it was simple to learn, compared to many other forms of writing that had thousands of symbols, and because the sea-faring Phoenicians brought it from place to place, the alphabet quickly became the basis for other languages.

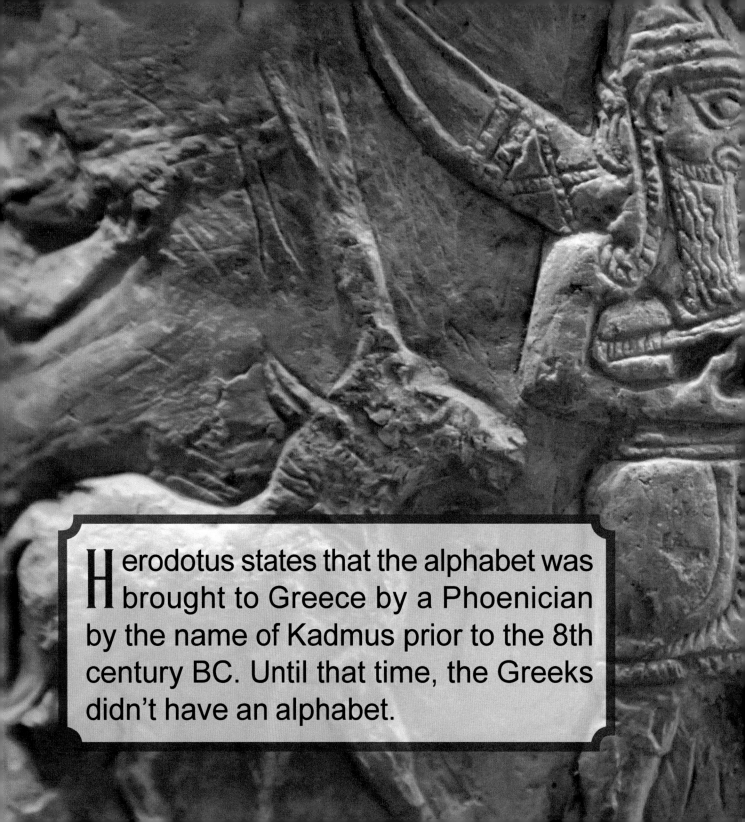

Herodotus states that the alphabet was brought to Greece by a Phoenician by the name of Kadmus prior to the 8th century BC. Until that time, the Greeks didn't have an alphabet.

BYBLOS HISTORICAL SITE

The Greeks called the religious city of Gebal, Byblos. The Greeks called the books of the Bible "Ta Biblia" for books, and this is where the Bible got its name. The population in Gebal

exported papyrus, called "bublos" in the Greek language, which was used to create scrolls of writing in ancient Greece.

ANCIENT PHOENICIAN MYTHS

Just as the Greeks adopted the Phoenician alphabet as their own, it's also thought that many of the Phoenician myths and their gods and goddesses were adapted and adopted by the Greeks. The story of the Phoenician gods Baal and Yamm bears a striking similarity to the story of the Greek god Zeus and his brother Poseidon. Even the battle between God and Satan in the Book of Revelation in the Bible shares some similarities.

THE MYTH OF BAAL AND YAMM

B aal was one of the most worshipped gods in the Phoenician religion. He was the son of El, who was the supreme god. Baal was the lord of the Earth and also of the rain.

BAAL

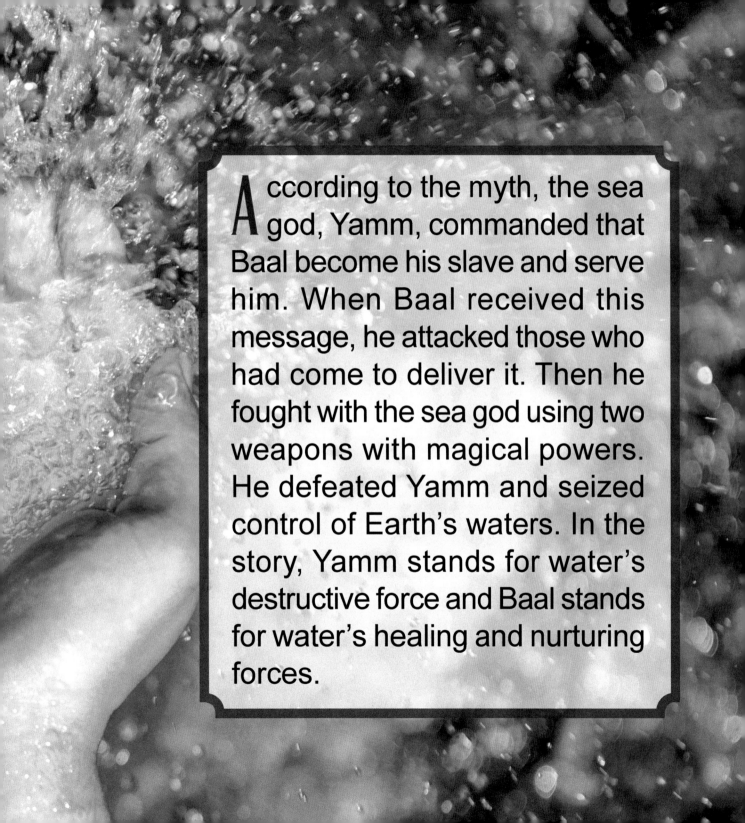

According to the myth, the sea god, Yamm, commanded that Baal become his slave and serve him. When Baal received this message, he attacked those who had come to deliver it. Then he fought with the sea god using two weapons with magical powers. He defeated Yamm and seized control of Earth's waters. In the story, Yamm stands for water's destructive force and Baal stands for water's healing and nurturing forces.

BAAL DOES BATTLE WITH MOT

After Baal won the battle with Yamm, he complained to his father El that he didn't have a fine house like the other gods, so El had Kothar, the god of crafts, build him a beautiful

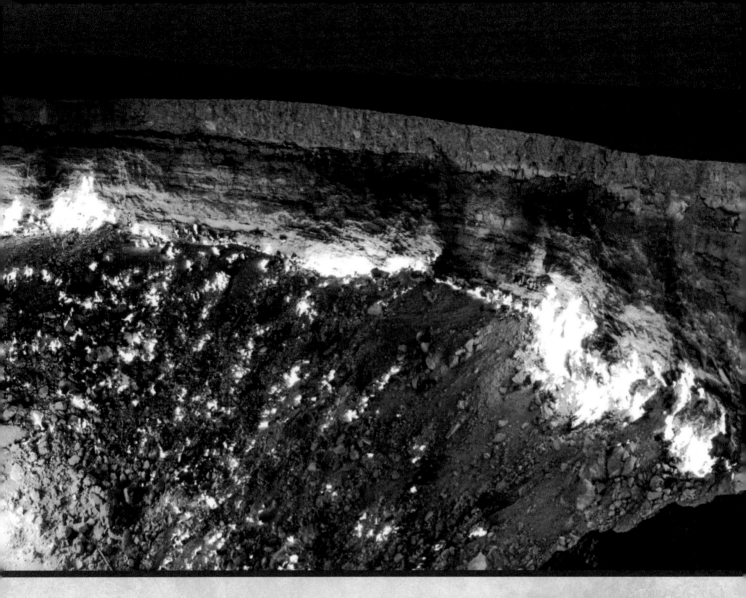

house. Baal had a feast to celebrate and invited all the gods, except for Mot, the god of death. Mot was offended so he asked that Baal join him for dinner in the Underworld.

Of course, Baal didn't want to go but he knew that he would once again offend Mot if he didn't, so he went. Mot served mud to Baal and with this food of death in his stomach, Baal was trapped down in the Underworld. Without Baal to bring fertility to the Earth, great famines gripped the land.

However, this wasn't the end of the story. Baal's wife was Anat and she was a powerful goddess. She went down to the Underworld and split Mot with a sword. Then she took his pieces and blew wind upon them to separate out the chaff. She burned Mot's pieces, then used a mill to grind them, and planted the ground-up pieces into the soil. Her actions brought her husband and brother, Baal, back to life.

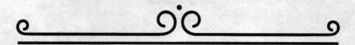

B aal eventually came back to his throne and the lands were fertile again. Mot also came back to life and the two fought once more. In this myth, Mot represents drought and Baal represents the springtime rains. The actions that Anat takes represent the process farmers use to harvest the crop of wheat.

CANAAN IN THE BIBLE

In the Old Testament, the civilization of Phoenicia is called "Canaan." This is the land where Moses led his people, the Israelites, when they escaped from Egypt.

EX

AUTHOR: Moses

DATE: 1420 or 1220 B.C.

CONTENT: Exodus deals with Moses' acceptance of God's people to freedom. God Pharaoh refused to let the last plague the Israelite

events that set Israel apart as a nation. First
structions to return to Egypt in order to le
devastating plagues upon Egypt beca
The ceremony of Passover
tion for all time of G
the Red Sea

It's also the land that Moses's successor Joshua conquered according to the Book of Exodus, although there isn't any archaeological support for this event.

Although the people in that region shared a common language, culture, and religious beliefs these Can'nai people didn't have a unified government.

The Phoenicians flourished despite the lack of unification and their maritime trade was at a height from 1500 to 332 BC when Alexander the Conqueror took over their major cities. After his death, the region became a battleground and his generals fought each other for power. Goods and artifacts from the ancient Phoenicians have been discovered as far away as Britain.

PHOENICIAN DESIGNS

THE PHOENICIANS
LEBANON - 1800 B.C.

FIRST ALPHABET
LEBANON - 1300 B.C.

IN CONCLUSION...

The Phoenician Civilization began before 3200 BC and had its height between 1500 to 332 BC. The Phoenicians created the first alphabet, which was given to the Greeks and became the basis for modern alphabets and phonics. Their purple dye colored the robes of important kings and they traveled the Mediterranean Sea and mapped it as they sailed in their beautifully decorated ships. Their myths influenced the mythology and beliefs of the Greeks. They traded their goods all over the Mediterranean world.

Awesome! Now that you've read about the Phoenician Civilization, you may want to read about another ancient civilization in the Baby Professor book *Olmec Civilization for Kids*

Made in the USA
Las Vegas, NV
27 February 2024

86394408R00040